MW00885705

MY FIRST BOOK
AUSTRALIA

ALL ABOUT AUSTRALIA FOR KIDS

GL🌐BED
CHILDREN BOOKS

Copyright 2023 by Globed Children Books

All rights reserved. No part of this book may be reproduced or distributed in any form without prior written permission from the author, with the exception of non-commercial uses permitted by copyright law.

Limited of Liability/Disclaimer of Warranty: The publisher and author make no representations or liabilities with respect to the accuracy and completeness of the contents of this work and specifically disclaim all warranties including without limitations warranties of fitness of particular purpose. No warranty may be created or extended by sales or promotional materials. This work is sold with the understanding that the publisher and author is not engaging in rendering medical, legal or any other professional advice or service. Further, readers should be aware that websites listed in this work may have changed or disappeared between when this work was written and when it is read.

Interior and cover Design: Daniel Day
Editor: Margaret Bam

For My Sons, Daniel, David and Jude

Melbourne Flinders Street Train Station

Australia

Australia is a **country**.

A country is land that is controlled by a **single government**. Countries are also called **nations, states, or nation-states**.

Countries can be **different sizes**. Some countries are big and others are small.

The Twelve Apostles, Australia

Where Is Australia?

Australia is geographically located in the continent of Australia.

A continent is a massive area of land that is separated from others by water or other natural features.

The country of Australia occupies the entire mainland of the Australian continent, which is located in the southern hemisphere of the world.

Australian Parliament House, Canberra

Capital

The capital of Australia is **Canberra.**

Canberra is located on the **southeastern part** of the country.

Sydney is also the largest city in Australia.

Gold Coast, Queensland, Australia

States

Australia is divided into six states and two territories.

The states of Australia are

New South Wales, Queensland, South Australia, Tasmania, Victoria, and Western Australia.

The two territories of Australia are

Australian Capital Territory (ACT) and the Northern Territory.

Population

Australia has population of around **26 million people.**

Australia is the most populated country in the continent of Australia and the 53rd most populated country in the world.

Sydney is the most populated city in Australia, with a population of over 5 million people. Around 85% of Australians live in urban areas, with the remaining 15% living in rural areas.

The Rocks, Sydney, Australia

Size

Australia is the largest country in the continent of Australia.

Australia is **7,692,024 km2** making it the 6th largest country in the world.

Australia is known for its diverse landscape, which includes deserts, mountains, rainforests, and beaches.

Languages

The national language of Australia is English. English is the most spoken language in the world with over a billion speakers.

Here are some Australian phrases
- Good on ya! - Well done; good stuff
- Having a whinge - To complain
- It's chockers in here - It's crowded in here
- Barbie - A barbecue

Sydney Opera House, Australia

Attractions

There are lots of interesting places to see in Australia.

Some beautiful places to visit in Australia are

- Sydney Opera House
- Great Barrier Reef Marine Park
- Uluru-Kata Tjuta National Park
- Sydney Harbour Bridge
- Blue Mountains National Park
- Melbourne's Culture

George Street, Sydney, Australia

History of Australia

Australia has a rich and long history which can be traced back to the arrival of Indigenous Australians, who are believed to have inhabited the continent for at least 60,000 years prior to the arrival of Europeans.

In 1770, the British navigator James Cook claimed the east coast of Australia for Great Britain, and in 1788 the First Fleet of British ships arrived in Sydney Cove, establishing the colony of New South Wales.

Customs in Australia

Australia has many fascinating customs and traditions.

- One of the most important celebrations in Australia is ANZAC Day. ANZAC Day is a national day of remembrance in Australia and New Zealand that commemorates the service and sacrifice of Australian and New Zealand soldiers who fought in World War I and subsequent conflicts.
- Australia is famous for its beaches. Many Australians enjoy swimming, surfing, and sunbathing at the beach.

Maitland, Australia

Music of Australia

Australia has a thriving music scene, with many talented musicians and bands. Popular music genres in Australia include Rock, Pop and Electronic Music.

Some notable Australian musicians include

- Iggy Azalea
- Sia
- Kylie Minogue
- Keith Urban
- Natalie Imbruglia

Vegemite on Bread

Food of Australia

Australian cuisine is a fusion of different cultures, including Indigenous Australian, British, European, and Asian influences.

Some popular dishes in Australia include

- **Meat Pies: A pastry shell filled with meat, usually beef, and gravy.**
- **Fish and Chips: Fried fish served with crispy chips.**
- **Tim Tams: Chocolate biscuits filled with chocolate cream and coated in chocolate.**
- **Vegemite on Toast: A breakfast spread made from yeast extract, often spread on buttered toast.**

Sorell, Australia

Weather in Australia

Australia is a very big country with lots of different kinds of weather. In the north, it's hot and sunny all year round, with tropical rainforests and beautiful beaches. In the south, it can get chilly in winter, with snow in the mountains and cooler temperatures. And in the middle, it's a desert with red sand and scorching hot days.

The hottest month in Australia is January.

Koala bear in Australia

Animals of Australia

There are many wonderful animals in Australia.

Here are some animals that live in Australia

- **Kangaroo**
- **Koala**
- **Marsupials**
- **Wombats**
- **Tasmanian devil**
- **Platypus**

Australia Rugby ball

Sports of Australia

Sports play an integral part in Australian culture. The most popular sports in Australia are **Australian Football, Rugby, Soccer and Cricket.**

Here are some of famous sportspeople from Australia

- **Cathy Freeman - Athletics**
- **Shane Warne - Cricket**
- **Ben Simmons - Basketball**
- **Don Bradman - Cricket**

Steve Irwin (1962-2006)

Celebrities

Australia has produced many notable figures

Here are some notable Australian figures

- **Steve Irwin - Zookeeper**
- **Liam Hemsworth - Actor**
- **Rebel Wilson - Actress**
- **Nicole Kidman - Actress**
- **Hugh Jackman - Actress**
- **Elle Macpherson - Model**
- **Iggy Azalea - Rapper**

Storybridge, Brisbane

Something Extra...

As a little something extra, we are going to share some lesser known facts about Australia

- **Australia has more than 10,000 beaches, which is more than any other country in the world.**
- **Australia is home to over 20,000 species of plants and animals that are found nowhere else in the world.**

Words From the Author

We hope that you enjoyed learning about the wonderful island of Australia.

Australia is a country rich in culture and beauty, with lots of wonderful places to visit and people to meet.

We hope you continue to learn more about this wonderful nation. If you enjoyed this book, consider leaving a review!

With Love

Made in United States
Orlando, FL
10 January 2025

57112037R00022